SHEETS OF GLASS

SHEETS OF GLASS

MARK HENDERSON

GOOSE LANE

© Mark Henderson, 1991.
All rights reserved. No part of this work may be reproduced or used in any form or by any means, electronic or mechanical, including photocopying, recording, or any information storage and retrieval system, without the prior written permission of the publisher. Requests for photocopying of any part of this book should be directed in writing to the Canadian Reprography Collective, 379 Adelaide Street West, Suite M1, Toronto, Ontario, Canada M5V 1S5.
Published with the assistance of the Canada Council and the New Brunswick Department of Tourism, Recreation and Heritage, 1991.

My writing has received continual support from several faculty members of the Department of English at the University of New Brunswick, Fredericton. Consequently, I thank Dr. Robert Gibbs, for his encouragement and guidance; Dr. Peter Thomas, for his criticism and assistance; and Dr. William Bauer and Dr. Kent Thompson, who continue to offer advice when I need it. As well, I thank Barbara Henderson for her support while this book was being written. Some of the work in this book first appeared in *The Antigonish Review, The Cormorant, The Fiddlehead,* and *Whetstone.*

Book design by Julie Scriver.
Printed and bound in Canada by The Tribune Press.

Canadian Cataloguing in Publication Data

Henderson, Mark, 1962-
Sheets of glass

Poems.
ISBN 0-86492-095-4

I. Title.

PS8565.E62S52 1991   C811'.54   C91-097557-4
PR9199.3.H56S52 1991

Goose Lane Editions
361 Queen Street
Fredericton, New Brunswick
Canada E3B 1B1

To My Mother and Father

No honest poet can ever feel quite sure
of the permanent value of what he has
written: he may have wasted his time
and messed up his life for nothing.

> T.S. Eliot, *The Use of Poetry and
> The Use of Criticism*

Contents

Three lives 9
Last spike 10
Rails 11
Poaching 12
Eulogy 13
Love is a small gift 14
When she died 15
My mother 16
Stairsteps 18
Sea heather 19
Grandmother's handbones 20
Canadian Legion 21
Starling 22
Mountie knife 23
Seven poems for John
1. *John's parents* 24
2. *John's brother* 26
3. *The yard* 27
4. *John* 28
5. *The accident* 29
6. *The fence* 30
7. *Memory of things seen* 31
Underside of the wharf 32
Arcadia 33
Loyalist graveyard 34
Hunters 35
Hardware store 36
Saturday afternoon 1 37
Saturday afternoon 2 38
Saturday afternoon 3 39
Backshop 40

Wad of bills 42
Wedding photograph 43
Rituals 44
Lion's blood 45
Blacksmith 46
Scarecrow 47
Roof of the cab 48
Lull 49
Weir fisherman 50
Shine and wrinkle 51
Sign 52
A sixpack of beer 53
Cemetery beyond the beach 54
Sunday drive 55
Covered bridge 56
Trees on the cliff 57
barnaby head 58
New River Beach 59
Kingfisher 60
On a clear day 61
Morning mist 62
Silence is the sound 63
Time stumbles 64
Avalon 65

Three lives

When his father came home to change his pants,
flustered and grinning like he'd just said something silly
at a dinner party (though he'd never been to one),
the wounds through the holes at the knees and elbows were
    purple,
a cross between meat and clotting, healing ooze.

And the wharf became known as the place
where a man risked his life each day
(though his father carried a pen and clipboard),
where a man barely escaped a boom (its wires snapped),
from where he came home smelling of sweat and fishmeal
and, sometimes, blood.

And while his father was foreman at forty,
his grandfather ruled the crew at twenty-two
(his grandfather, with twelve starched white linen shirts,
and every sports coat and blazer with a pulled thread
known as *workclothes*, the only man who could cross his legs
and still look tough).

And his is a better life than both of these.
He'll never work with his hands
(though he's too bulky to sit at a desk,
and shirts and ties cut into him),
but late at night, he grows callouses on his fingertips
from squeezing a pen too tightly.

Last spike

Ribbon of iron, rusted with blood,
devil's paintbrush and alder's onslaught
have made you quaint.
The rolling wheel that keeps you burnished
in the memory of my father.
While the Atlantic breeze wiped the sweat
from his brow, he could lay his hand to steel
that pierced the hearts of B.C. coolies.

Tieplates from torn-up track
are bookends now, the alpha and omega
of the story of his life.
Remembrances colour my eyes,
hang larger than life in railway stations,
tributes to a man who could paint the night
and capture the sea's freedom.

The old man who piped the sun down ivory houses
is gone, but sandpipers still sing
glinting cuts in the waves' rhythmic wash
like the scrape of rough-knobbed hands and the whiskerburns
that are a child's legacies.

Rails

Rails lead out of town,
iron bands that held my father forty years.
When I was young and walking here,
rails could take me to the four corners of the earth,
even McAdam.
That was when I was young,
and rails had an end;
that was when it was summer,
and the days dragged on for hours.

These are the ties that bind:
you don't stop walking these rails
till you get off.
Red ants will eat you alive,
like they ate my father as he stood one place,
paid by the ton,
moving fishmeal and tin.

When I'm on rails at dusk and dawn,
I walk alone.
There's a bear in the woods, they say.
They're right: I saw his footprints in the sand,
heard shadows crashing through underbrush.
But he must come out to face me
while I'm on rails.

Poaching

Five o'clock on Sunday morning,
mist rises from water like breath.
His father lies in ankle-deep water, bellyflat,
driving a sawed-off broomstick
topped with a tuna hook
under the lee of a boulder.

He sits on a small bluff,
the head of the beach.
Instead of watching for fisheries officers,
he watches his father walking over the water, knees high,
shaking out a burlap sack,
carrying a lobster like a banner,
its back arched passed the point of breaking
before snapping in on itself.

Later, he gives the lobster pencils to crush in its claws
and hears water begin to bubble on the stove.
He wonders why he is the only one his father takes poaching,
and he is proud.

Eulogy

I write my father's eulogy
before his memory fades into abstracts,
while the brooding hens of arthritis
still lay eggs, nestled and swollen,
at his wrists and knees, joints that crack
with the sound of tiny, chipping beaks.

He could have been a doctor
or a lawyer; he could have sat
monocled on a high stool,
blending springs and diamonds
in the works of a watch.

Given the choice,
maybe he *would* have spent his days
tying knots in his fingers, carving
weatherlines in his face, shaping
a dockworker out of himself.

But he never had the chance
to choose, buckled under
by a wife, nine children,
and other kinds of debt.

Love is a small gift

Love is a small gift passed
between my father and me:

a jackknife of German steel,
rosewood and brass
that he keeps in the medicine cabinet,
afraid to lose it;

a bowl of fiddleheads,
the green of unseen riverbanks,
steaming on a sunlit table.

When she died

When she died, he seeded the garden with grass,
running the mower over the ground
where peas grew, and where his children,
green in their pods, ate their fill.

He claimed he was not a gardener,
that the mould of the earth
choked his throat, filled his lungs,
as he tore up the plants that ringed the house.

Though he swore he'd never grow
another flower, that summer the cosmos
he'd missed sprang up overhead,
pansies blossomed in a circle through the lawn,
and poplar stakes that held the raspberry canes
sprouted leaves.

My mother

In the grey days, my mother was an obelisk,
by height and breadth the twin of the wringer washer
she fed with our clothes
(while she pinned pants and shirts and longjohns
against the sky, I leaned across the machine's hum
and dared my fingers to tease the wooden rollers).

She was a lump of stone at the edge of the playground;
the whole overcast sky funneled down on the hump
of her back, a small, hunched figure supporting
the roof of the world, her presence protecting me
like a medal or a millstone around my neck.

Now her body is burned to ashes (the fat ones burn
better they say, a candle effect, a wick of porous bone),
a box of pale crumbs and dust committed to the sea
(she left a fine white mantle upon the water,
refusing to sink).

And only now I think of the day at the beach
with her sister, whose lips left red stains
on the filters of her cigarettes, of the blue-veined
deltas of my mother's thighs, white, broad and pitted:

> I waded out with them, behind them,
> until I was up to my neck, on tiptoe,
> afraid to lose my grip on the soft mud.

> And then she was swimming away
> from where I stood heavy,
> my face slapped by the waves.

Deep in her breaststroke,
she was free of the earth,
she was weightless,
she was flying.

Stairsteps

Here he can see the road
hidden in straw and goldenrod,
and they come from yesterday,
his mother, brothers and sisters, himself.

Her legs brush thistles aside,
legs speckled and brown,
the shine of patent leather,
the colour of the wooden newel post
at the foot of the stairs,

her children behind her,
youngest to oldest,
children like stairsteps,
going up.

Sea heather

A breeze blows the scent of sea heather,
elusive as a remembered whisper,
across a saltmarsh:

again I see my mother
hanging bundles of flowers
from backporch windows,
so little they give
only the impression of mauve.

Grandmother's handbones

Our grandmother's handbones
are delicate trellises
sprayed with ivy, violet-vined,
spread with gossamer
when she holds them to the sun.

Canadian Legion

Growing up in a big family,
he knows only two people:
brother and not-brother
(the one he turns away from
when a weakness is found and gouged).

He does not know why
he deliberately slows his pace crossing
the Canadian Legion dance hall floor,
letting the man from Backbay
punch his brother three more times,
held by the arms.

Starling

He was one of the children crying for a young, brown starling
when the boys beat the grey, shingled eaves
with long poles. But he couldn't keep the bird
in a cardboard box in the backporch without feeling the dying
as he watched the pulse of the head.

By evening light he hung by the dead skin of his knees
to the rusted nails in the wall of the barn,
forcing the bird into the nest,
the blue mother pecking until their blood mixed,
until there was just a boy on a barn,
a body in the eaves.

Mountie knife

If there is a god,
I am damned:
not for the rum nights
or the Christ jokes
or the young backseats;

but for the time when I was seven years old:
I drove the big blade of my mountie knife
through the thick skull of a great-horned,
bulging-eyed, big-lipped sculpin,
not understanding his ugliness.

The hum of his vibrating body
sang through the haft and up my arm;
he sings his life out
now.

Seven poems for John

1. John's parents

I cannot remember John
without seeing his father
running neighbourhood kids
out of his yard,
waving a yardstick over his head,
shouting, *I bea'choo! I bea'choo!*
A tape measure flutters
around his neck; he runs awkwardly
in black shiny dress shoes and glossy pants,
never able to catch us,
though he might not have wanted to.

I try to pull other images
of John's parents out of my head
like pictures from a family album,
but they are all drab, oppressive.
Their clothes are always grey or black,
heavy. Their shoes,
even his mother's,
large and unattractive, sturdy,
utilitarian.

I remember his father's drooping mustache,
his forehead running down
to a permanent, frowning brow.

I remember the plainness
of his mother's face, the tightness of her hair
pulled back to a netted bun.
I do not remember seeing them smile,
and my imagination cannot
create smiles for them.

2. John's brother

Joseph's hair sits high on his crown,
bushes out straight from his forehead;
large fishlike lips are parted
by thick square teeth; ears hang
like jug handles; eyes bulge,
the lids fat and heavy.
Joseph has a mole on his face,
though I do not remember where.

His skin seems powdered
with a fine yellow dust:
it is always a surprise
that his cheeks do not stain
dark when the tears finally come;
instead, the drops run palely
over his smooth, rounded face.

Joseph is a wooden caricature
of a boy, come suddenly to life:
like his mother, he wears square
dull shoes, and long into the fall
he dresses in shorts
and high heavy socks;
his smile is painted on,
and he runs and skips with a tug
and a jerk, as if he dangles
from the strings of a puppeteer.

3. *The yard*

The house is tiny and shingled
with a bowed peak, as if squashed
by larger buildings on either side.
Downstairs is their father's tailor shop;
the family lives above. Out back,
the grass ends twenty feet
from the house, replaced by hard dry earth
and large concrete slabs.

The sun always seems hottest
on this tiny desert, and even the most humid days
seem not to disturb the aridity
of this little stretch of barren soil.
It is here that John and Joseph
make a small clubhouse
from plywood and old crates.

Shortly before supper, their mother leans
out the door and speaks curtly in Hungarian
to Joseph, a woman who has learned that orders
are respected more than requests.

4. John

John is short and strong and waddles
when he walks. He is dressed in ugly
greens and browns, turtlenecks and
heavy corduroys, even in the middle
of summer. His head is large, oblong,
his bottom lip a wet undercarriage
for his lolling tongue. I bring candy;
we sit alone in the clubhouse,
where he unwraps his caramels
with stubby fingers. While he chews,
complacency settles on his face;
every physical sensation is
a source of meditation for him,
a solemn occasion. He whispers secrets,
though I do not understand a word he says.

5. The accident

It was nothing, says Joseph,
*we were wrestling and John pushed me
backwards.* John plays with a small
ambulance, not seeming to hear. He pushes
the toy along slowly, putting his weight
on it to make tracks in sand
heaped on the concrete. *We fell over
together; I hit my head on that block.*
The block's corner is brown, the block
sits in a dried brown pool; smaller drops
lead out of the clubhouse. Joseph's voice
is hoarse with a story told many times but
not believed. I try to imagine a steel clamp
biting his skull beneath his ball cap,
biting deep into his thinking.

6. The fence

After the accident, children are not allowed
in the yard; it becomes a game for us,
entering the yard under an assumed innocence,
to be chased out minutes later, the tailor's
fists shaking, his face white. He screams
in a hard language we do not understand;
then comes the inevitable, *I bea'choo!*
I bea'choo! We come for the spectacle of the chase.

Finally, he builds a high chain-link fence
around the yard; Joseph is given
his freedom;
we lose interest. But sometimes
I sneak through the backyards
in twilight, poke my head through the hedgerow;
John runs to me, low-sweeping
feet swishing and snapping the grass.
With a handful of caramels, we sit side by side,
leaning our shoulders against each other
through the diamond links; we unwrap each candy
and eat it slowly, John a little Buddha beside me,
his legs crossed, his fat little belly
with its popped button sticking out beneath
his sweater. Black veins of sand flow
in the creases of his skin. I rise to go
and he stands, fingers clenching fence wire,
his face so perfectly unaccusing that I hang
my head in shame and skulk away.

7. Memory of things seen

I do not remember precisely when
John's family moved away.
At some point the tailor changed
from the comic, crazy Hungarian;
now he shakes not with rage
but with fear. And most of all
I see the fence: the posts
ended in angled bars at the top,
bars strung with barbed wire.

And for the first time I realize
that those bars were not angled out,
to keep us from getting in;
they were angled in,
to keep John from getting out.
And to this day I see him at the fence
with an innocent, contemplative look
on his face and me turning my back
on him to cut through
the backyards toward home.

Underside of the wharf

Our idea of hell is the underside of the wharf,
where the sun never shines,
where all you hear is the drip of seawater,
barnacles and periwinkles shifting inside shells,
and the booming coo of pigeons
roosting at the top of creosoted pilings.

Standing on the landing pontoon at lowtide,
you can almost jump to the rock cradles.
We live down here all summer,
jigging crabs from the bottom
and fishing harbour pollock with mussels
we pull from the bottom of the pontoon,

until the day we reach into the sparkling cold
up to our shoulders, yank on some kelp,
and the man who went missing in the coldest month
comes gliding out from under, hand first,
like he just came up to say *hello*.

Arcadia

On the night of the graduation dance,
he backed out of the car door
and saw himself in the curve
of a rearview mirror:

> hair and socks
> and shoes, a pot-
> belly and pointed
> ears, legs narrowing
> into little black
> hooves.

The moon flayed the darkness from them
like a raw, black skin, and the poplars
turned up their silver palms and whispered
among themselves.

Loyalist graveyard

When they found the dockworker's son
in the backseat with the daughter of summer people,
and found that children had killed
the grass in a path to the only beach
where they could swim without sneakers
to keep rocks and clamshells
from cutting their feet,
the people on the hill wanted to build a fence
around the knoll.

                In the Loyalist graveyard
next to the dedicated high school,
boys plotted buying gasoline early,
and saving rags and bottles,
and what they could do with gunpowder
emptied from shotgun shells,
while men with families hoped
they would hire locals to dig postholes,
pour cement, staple the wire.

Hunters

Hoofprints worked deep in the mud
were left by the buck jumping straight up
through brush, breaking into an open field.
Your gun at the back of his head
never fires as you see him go down
at the sound of your partner's rifle.

He rises up to sprawl headlong,
tongue lolling, eyes rolling,
shot a second time,
now through the neck.

The deer isn't big enough
for the Big Buck Contest
he wants to win.
Your tag through his ear,
a voice not your own says,
I want the antlers, then.

And you parade him around as your own,
as if no one knows who's done the killing,
two of three cartridges given by a brother
tucked at the back of a nightstand drawer.

Gutting the buck,
you find he ran sixty yards,
shot through the heart.
You saw through his brain and sinus passages
to take the antlers,
avoiding his stare.

Hardware store

When he was a crow of a child,
glittering things attracted him:
goldfish, red devils, and spinners
lured more hours than fish.
Every box on a shelf in his mind,
he created the most wonderful tacklebox,
while the fat Englishman
leaned on the paintshaker,
waiting for him to steal.

When he was eighteen and working there,
he wrote a letter about the fifty dollars
he stole from the till.
When the owner called out to the backshop
for the boy to come in from the cold
and to tell him he had character,
he couldn't stop stacking kegs of nails
with gloveless hands, punching them into place,
driving threepennies through his palms,
and slivers of softwood under his nails.

Saturday afternoon 1

He looks like Santa's elf:
squat, bowlegged, barrel-shaped;
the only tufts of hair shoot up
and out just above his ears.

His boots are still wet from the beach;
I look at the manager until he nods
and charge the insulated rubber gloves.
I write his name on the bill and say it's familiar.

Well-mannered, helpful, innocent, he says,
I'm the one who killed my wife.
I raise my eyebrows
and nod in polite recognition.

Saturday afternoon 2

He comes to town on Saturday,
stows his beer in the cool,
mud-floor cellar of the store,
where shards of glass
and mirror sparkle more than the spring
that cuts a channel
from corner to corner.

I measure, score, and cut
sheets of glass while he sits
with his beer on the third step up.
He left school in grade two;
for some reason, I speak loud, slow,
simple.

He glances at an uneven rock wall,
where my shadow and the shadow of my tools move,
the glass casting nothing, making it seem
I only go through the motions of work.
He sighs and climbs the stairs, an old man
who beat his wife to death
and threw her body in a gully.

Saturday afternoon 3

His girlfriend has tears that move
across the eye instead of out.

He is in jail again.

He came home to find
his son-in-law had stove in
the four sides of his one-room house,
clapboarded and whitewashed,
with an axe and a crowbar.
His boat was sunk, his outboard
thrown overboard. With the same crowbar,
he beat his son-in-law,
breaking his ribs and his back.

It is a quiet
Saturday afternoon.
In the cellar
I measure, score, and cut
sheets of glass.

Backshop

There are times
when a backshop
seems larger than before,

when a fat man
from Newcastle-on-Tyne
with a pin-cushion nose
is the only one there,

and the only sound
is the buzzing of the lights,

and he tells you
he was walking
through a field with his girl
when the planes flew over London;

after, all she could say was
What language came from you!

There are times
when a man
who likes his Scotch too much
will fix you with red-welled eyes
and say that,
           after the bomb,
he couldn't tell
the mother from the baby
smeared along a red brick wall.

There are times
when the buzz of the lights
is too loud, and the feelers
at the edges of your mind
can't get over the size of the room.

Wad of bills

The wad of bills under the counter
is for men who will never
get a loan at a bank,
especially for a flat of beer,
a bottle of wine, or a new clam hoe.

There is no interest
unless you count
the quartercord of fine, hard, stove wood
the lender finds in his backyard
or a bucket of clams left on his doorstep,
wet, blueblack, and living.

Wedding photograph

Standing on that bridge
in the park, starched
tuxedo collar chafing
his neck, he remembers
catching frogs here as a boy,

that even now, bats are roosting
under the planks
at their feet, delicate wings
holding the fine, soft sheen
of an old man's skin.

Rituals

The gladiola do their dueling
in the summer garden pit.
When they die from the strain of violent colours,
their stalks are gently plucked,
their bulbs unearthed.

The old man will smile at the roots
drying in his shed,
like a man with a pocketful of dragon's teeth.

Violets and pansies growing through the lawn
stand pensively with lowered faces,
as if contemplating a seasonal beheading,
intent on something in the grass.

Lion's blood

He contracted polio when he was eight.

His simple brother (who school children looked at strangely
when they walked by, a cigarette in his hand,
gazing thoughtfully at a pull-toy row of yellow ducks,
string dangling from nicotine fingers),
his simple brother pulled him in a red wagon,
then pushed him in a wheelchair.

On good days, when he walked with a cane
and took off the black glove of his left hand,
he painted oil Tarzans on stretched canvases.
Sitting on his verandah, squinting from the dimness of our
    small sun,
he painted the flesh tones of an Englishman in African daylight,
mixing his bases to the colour of lion's blood.

Blacksmith

He claimed
> he was a hundred and thirty-two years old,
> conceived when his mother walked barefoot
> on a heath of mayflowers.

But
> when Sunday morning found him
> sprawled backwards over the chain
> that protected the post office grass,
> smelling of the water of life,
>
> the town's last blacksmith
> hung like an old, carelessly dropped sackcloth,
> newly fallen from the sky.

Scarecrow

He led a banker's life at an early age
in a Cape Cod house between the deacon and the doctor.
The town grew used to his aquiline ways
and how he sneered a smile from his teeth
as if his lips were stuck in place.
He never stood without turning a calf
and spoke with eloquence against a fashionable outrage.

When his wife left, he looked straight ahead,
voiced no opinion, worked in his garden on the hottest days,
sat with his shotgun and protected his seed,
hung crows by the heels from his bean poles with lace.

Roof of the cab

The roof of the cab shows at halftide
under the water; all the men on the dock
know and nod. When the diver hooks it
to the winch, the old man cannot stop mumbling,
That's not his truck,
as it comes dripping up from the bottom,
his son's knuckles skinned
from punching windows watered tight.

And as the mumbles grow to a voice
deep, hard, and telescoped,
no one stops to think
that no one argues back.

Lull

The day they chose to seine the weir was dark and overcast;
a ripple stole across the seagrass, wild raspberry canes,
and morning glories. The cool of silver upturned leaves
shone on poplar branches, and the cove broke its colour
to brown, blue and green; gulls in trances of seafree whitecaps
heard the cursing benedictions of men straining
on a hundred hogshead of glittering herring.
The rain was featherwarm and just as light, settling carefully
on the curve of forearm hair and nesting in cracks of salt-red
    hands.

Fish-rich and weather-blessed, a deck hand sees
a smiling frown beneath the charcoaled and furrowed brow
of clouds that peer over the edge of the dusky hills,
the cloudface of a boy about to knock down
carefully placed soldiers in mock battle.

Weir fisherman

When he jigs a dogfish caught in the weir,
he holds her down with a boot
and rips her swollen white belly open
for being what she is. They slide out,
wet, grey, and alive.

Tourists with ten dollar bills
and formaldehyde jars
wait on the wharf for boats to come in.
He rows to the net and throws out
the little sharks that nip his fingers.

Shine and wrinkle

Chalkwhite houses stand unpainted
on the fisherman's side, baring silver shingles
shimmering translucent to the clear wood beneath.
Slender yards run to the breakwaters,
carefully mowed plantain, dandelion, and clover.

The sun strong-arms its way through low, blue hills,
sends rays racing low over the water
toward the boat like a flock of gulls.
The diesel throb pushes open a plastic kitchen curtain:
tea kettle steam rises against the sunlight of a far window.

The stumps of a dozen rum wharves bob and flash
like seal heads. The fisherman leans low over
the gunwale and lets the water's shine and wrinkle
burn its reflection in his face.

Sign

On the one-hundred-twentieth day without work
he took his coffee down to the beach,
where the beans' oil settled in continents
in his cup, and high, thin clouds
drifted across the surface
of a black, liquid world.

He had lost faith;
even the gulls were silent and solitary
at this time of day;
the ducks skated, together but separate,
on the distant sun's reflected sparkle.

He lay down on the bank,
let the green earth swallow him up.
It welcomed him but would not let him rest:
purple-headed tallgrass tickled at his arms;
wild rice, lime with new leaf, whispered in scarlet stems;
and the sweet, ripe smell of wild strawberries
hiding in the grass made him drunk.

What restored him was none of these;
it was that, while he lay there,
he heard the swoop of waxy wings majestic
where no bird was.
That it was only an osprey above his brow
or a crow beneath his cheekbones
made no difference.
He had been given a sign;
he rose.

A sixpack of beer

When a man is too far out
of town, a sixpack of beer means
everything, just as a man
who steals bottles from the back of a truck
must get his brothers when he is accused
of stealing and come back to the camp,

just as a man keeps getting up
as a brother keeps hitting him
with a tire iron, screeching
stay down, you bastard, stay down.

Cemetery beyond the beach

In the twilight of bonfires
and minds as far away as stars,
the shadows of night's edge
fall with heavier feet.
In this fog made thick with particles
of light, you might rub shoulders
with a boy killed by a falling spar,
as you rest your hand on his granite tombstone,
rough and warm in the cool white down.

In the murmuring dawnlight
that intrudes like a hesitant memory,
wisps of mist cling to the shrouds
of a fading squarerigger,
blurring the lines
between myth and remembrance.

Sunday drive

You need the sky
funneled in like this,
the river valley
not the be-all,
but just the edge
of something else.

The farm is real
after watching scenery
roll by on a canvas:

in this sunlight,
bleached shingles bristle,
spokes on the harvester
stand independent of the hub;

wizard trees hunch round the yard,
intent on their magic,
while behind them the river
swirls like a dragon,
shines like a pearl.

Covered bridge

They built the covered bridge so that two chariots
might pass easily; none of the builders had ever seen
a chariot, unless Macaulay or Webster
illustrated one.

Timbers, planks and principles
old as the Roman arch
gave the bridge resilience
and solid strength
belied by the filtered sunlight
sifting through the cracks.
Rotted wood was replaced by new;
pied grey and fresh tawny
combined like the smells of horses
and applecarts rumbling through.

The covered bridge was razed,
replaced by iron rods and concrete;
the new bridge crumbles
before all natural things
and will fall in the Stillwater someday,
losing a family of swallows to the undertow.

Trees on the cliff

Here on the first spur, the proud
proceed in a slow and patient suicide
toward the cliff's edge.
Blasted and white, stripped of bark,
their roots cling with swollen knuckles.

They move on a mat of rusted copper,
where lichens crystallize
into tiny patina chalices.
They are transfixed by sun and water,
by islands floating like puffs of clouds
in the distant air.

On the islands, the trees are a living green,
though the red sandstone
gives way beneath their feet,
falling, leaving the trees
twisting upward in silent survival,
gnarled to perfection.

barnaby head

returning from barnaby head,
i remember these things only:

> the bell buoy's toll,
> the size of the seaducks,
> twelve blue iris infused
> in a crotch of land,
> how well the sea captured
> the artist's impression,
>
> and, how walking to the tip
> and turning inward,
> i saw a thin red line
> running through the rockface.

New River Beach

Thinking so lightly he leaves no bootprints,
the boy stands at the tide's latest lapmark.
Rocks make trails in the sand
like comets.

And though he'll take the open mussel
found sparkling violet-blue fading to black,
he can't take his eyes off the waves:
    to be that water,
    forever riding
    on the point of breaking to white,
    to leave a seashell sitting brimful
    in the sand, while clamholes
    blow kisses in the backwash.

Kingfisher

        He is a mote in the eye,
        a stutter of skylight momently folded on itself,
        a dark hair wavering in the midair of evening.

And then

        He lilts in the ether,
        hesitates and dives into the dark salt water,
        rises up and wings toward you,
        a winking navel,
        a dimple in the dusk that draws in the universe.

On a clear day

At a mile, the gulls are only flecks of white,
kites that rise and fall,
rise and fall against the island cliffs;
they disappear in the cool, Sinbad shadows,
reappear against the Ali Baba red sandstone,
against the Peter Pan green that drips like frosting
down towards the shore.

                    Irridescent, treeless,
the Brothers sprawl like two pods, side by side,
but through the summer air bleeds the cry of the blackbacks.

They are slaughtering ducklings.

One by one they swoop amid the frantic peeps,
the tiny flapping of half-formed wings,
an image instantly echoed in the too-still water.

The eiders swim to each new attack,
powerful, helpless,
then patiently wait in stoic silence,
engulfed in a murder of innocents,
with no arms to cradle their young.

Morning mist

Rising mist breaks the moving heart,
steaming up from the sweating fronds
of dusty roadside weeds.

Breaking mist moves the rising heart,
bursting out of the early morning mouths
of hornless deer.

Moving mist raises the breaking heart,
curling up out of the calm river's mouth,
dreaming a cloud dream.

Silence is the sound

Silence is the sound
the breaking heart takes,
splintering down to the green,
cool lume of new wood,
deep to the core of an older beam,
until scalloped edges meet and match
the sound of noiseless echoes.

Time stumbles

Now and then
time stumbles,
leaves a part
of itself
like the skin
of a scraped knee
on a sidewalk,
like the air
in a parlour,
dim and cool
and stale.

Avalon

Like a water balloon bloating with a sudden squeeze,
I feel the bulk of my life
shift with each new passage,
and I think *Maybe this time it will take shape.*

Perhaps in the final second of death
the moulding will be done,
or will I drift off in a boat of afterlife,
pushed through another narrows,
my future bulging on a distant island?